Starting
Ukulele

The number one method for
young ukulele players

by Steven Sproat

WISE PUBLICATIONS
part of The Music Sales Group
London / New York / Paris / Sydney / Copenhagen / Berlin / Madrid / Tokyo

Notes to students and teachers

Dedication
To Harry Hill, for giving me the confidence to do this.

Acknowledgements
I would like to thank my dad who bought me my first uke when I was about ten and faithfully took me to Blackpool three times a year to watch players and pick up tips from the George Formby Society. I would also like to thank Derek, who encouraged me as an early teen and sent me songs to try, and Stephen Helme and Peter Moss – both of whom I still admire and whose work demonstrates the reasons why I'm passionate about the ukulele. In addition, thanks goes to my daughter Gabrielle for helping me with this book and for her determination as a new uke player.

Finally I would like to thank you for buying the book. I hope it encourages you to go further than you thought possible... go for it!

To get the best out of this book & CD, you will need a soprano ukulele in the common C tuning. Notes are given on the CD to help you tune your instrument (see page 9).

The main idea for the book & CD is to make playing the ukulele fun, to help you learn quickly, and to get you playing some good tunes. You don't have to be able to read music to use this book – we'll take you right from the beginning!

So now, grab your uke and get ready to have some fun!

With thanks to Hanks Guitar Shop, London.

Published by
Wise Publications
14-15 Berners St, London, W1T 3LJ, UK

Exclusive Distributors:
Music Sales Limited
Distribution Centre, Newmarket Road, Bury St Edmunds, Suffolk IP33 3YB, UK.
Music Sales Corporation
257 Park Avenue South, New York, NY10010, USA.
Music Sales Pty Limited
20 Resolution Drive, Caringbah, NSW 2229, Australia.

Order No. AM990286
ISBN 978-1-84772-049-8
This book © Copyright 2007 Wise Publications,
a division of Music Sales Limited

Project editor: Rachel Payne
Original design: Kathy Gammon
Cover design and layout: Fresh Lemon
Photography: Matthew Ward
Models: Garth Amos, Rémy Le Berre, Daisy Lloyd & Gabrielle Sproat
Pictures courtesy of: Hulton Archive/Getty Images.

Printed in China.

Your Guarantee of Quality
As publishers, we strive to produce every book to the highest commercial standards. The music has been freshly engraved and the book has been carefully designed to minimise awkward page turns and to make playing from it a real pleasure. Particular care has been given to specifying acid-free, neutral-sized paper made from pulps which have not been elemental chlorine bleached. This pulp is from farmed sustainable forests and was produced with special regard for the environment. Throughout, the printing and binding have been planned to ensure a sturdy, attractive publication which should give years of enjoyment. If your copy fails to meet our high standards, please inform us and we will gladly replace it.

www.musicsales.com

Contents

The wonderful world of ukes

(1) You've made an excellent choice in taking up the ukulele – it is fun, cool and once you've got started who knows where it might lead. Perhaps you have seen or heard The Ukulele Orchestra Of Great Britain, bought a ukulele from a music shop or people around you have started to play. Whatever the reason, through this book I'd like to help you become familiar with your instrument.

One of the great things about the ukulele is that you don't need to be able to read music to play it. This doesn't mean that it isn't good to learn music theory (it's a great thing to understand musical principles) but you can start learning the ukulele without that knowledge. In this book I want to take a practical approach and we will look at some techniques and chords and a bit of the general background to the ukulele.

Instruments: Buying your ukulele or moving on from a budget one...

The saying 'you get what you pay for' is true for most of the things we buy in life and buying a ukulele is no exception – better instruments cost more money. However a good thing about the ukulele is that you don't have to spend a fortune on your instrument, there are many good quality ukuleles at the lower end of the market. These have come into the country in recent years through brands such as Mahalo, Lanikai, Vintage and Stagg, all offering ukuleles that are good value for money (starting from less than £15).

I was once told that you can only play as well as your instrument will allow you to play and I have learned that this is true. My playing radically improved when my dad bought me a decent uke – I started to love practising because it sounded so good! Don't struggle with a cheap instrument if it stops you from practising, experimenting, or if it seems like a 'workhorse'. But you don't need to buy an expensive instrument straight away – it is wise to invest in a good one once you have already learned the basics and feel comfortable with your playing ability and progression.

I recommend spending around £40 for a uke to learn on – this should serve you well for a couple of years as you begin to get to grips with the instrument. It needs to be set up correctly, have reliable tuning pegs and a good 'action' (this means the height the strings are away from the body and fretboard). If the action on the ukulele is too high it can usually be lowered, but take it to a music shop or guitar maker and seek guidance. All of this will get you off to a good start!

The uke family

 *Soprano*

 *Concert*

 *Tenor*

 *Baritone*

Soprano

The soprano ukulele is the most popular and common size of ukulele – the 'standard' size. It is the soprano ukulele we will be learning about in this book, and it is generally tuned to the notes G, C, E and A.

Concert

The concert ukulele is larger in body size and length than the soprano ukulele. This gives extra width between the frets (useful if you've big fingers!). It sounds slightly louder and is a little bit more mellow. It is also normally tuned to the notes G, C, E and A.

Tenor

The tenor ukulele is often used for complicated solo playing in an approach quite similar to the classical guitar. I've heard it used for jazz and classical pieces where very accurate and complex chords are required. It is bigger than the concert ukulele, about half the size of the guitar, and is normally tuned to the notes G, C, E and A.

Baritone

This is the biggest ukulele and it is regularly tuned to D, G, B and E (it is in the key of G). These are the same notes as the highest four strings on the guitar.

What's a ukulele and what's a ukulele banjo?

I'm often asked this question. The ukulele banjo is a cross between a banjo and a ukulele. It is similar in length to a ukulele but has a banjo-type body and a vellum (skin). They both use the same tuning and are played in similar ways, although some strokes suit one instrument better than the other. Ukulele banjos are much louder than normal (Hawaiian) ukuleles and have a more abrasive tone. In the 1920–30s, before microphones were available, banjo ukes were popular because their sound would carry well in concerts and music halls.

The normal Hawaiian ukulele can create a greater variety of sound and has a soft, sweet tone that is very pleasant to listen to. This traditional instrument has become popular again, probably because you can play lots of different styles on it!

A few ideas you might find useful

Strings...

Strings are a very important part of your equipment. It is probably a good idea to carry a spare set in case one breaks when you're out playing. Ask at a music shop if you're unsure how to change your strings yourself.

If your budget for a new ukulele is limited to around £15 don't worry as there are some excellent strings called Aquila which make even a modest instrument sound good – put these on your uke and notice the difference!

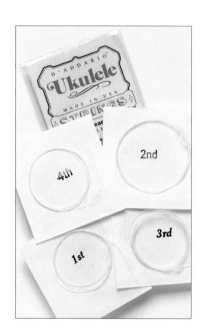

Metronome...

A metronome is a helpful gadget that helps you keep in time when you are learning to play. It's not essential but it might help – keeping in time is very important, especially with a rhythm instrument like the uke.

You can buy digital or mechanical metronomes. It doesn't matter which you get, but digital ones tend to be more portable and you may find that useful.

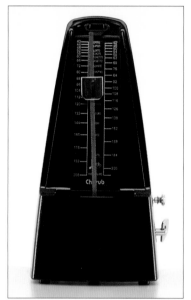

Uke chord dictionary...

You won't need all the chords in a chord dictionary overnight so please don't worry if it looks daunting! In this book I cover the most frequently used chords but if you want to play a pop song and use more unusual chords then it's handy to have a chord book.

Tuner...

It's a good idea to get hold of a tuner. Your playing will sound terrible if your ukulele is not in tune, however good you are! You can tune from the notes we give you on the CD, however it's handy to have something which you can use wherever you are. Some tuners fit on the end of your uke so you can see and tune at the same time.

Parts of the ukulele

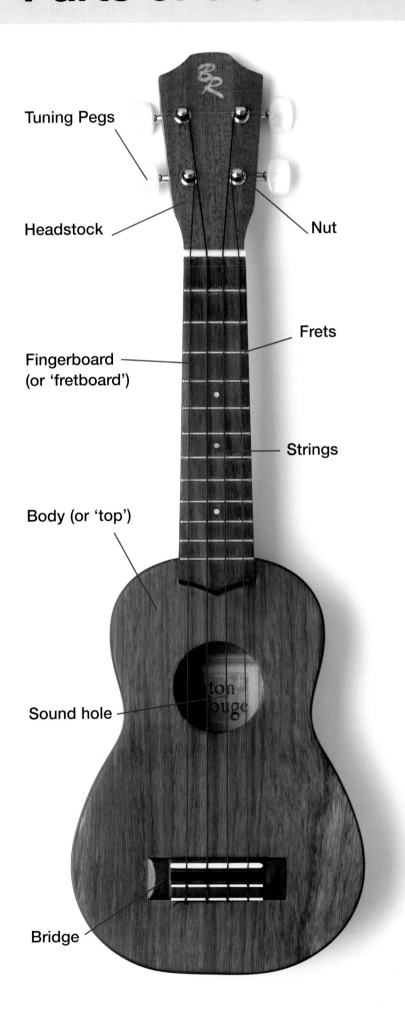

Tuning Pegs

Headstock

Nut

Frets

Fingerboard
(or 'fretboard')

Strings

Body (or 'top')

Sound hole

Bridge

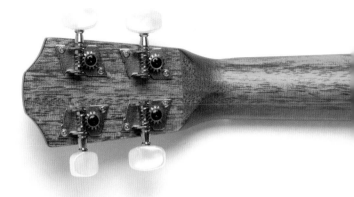

The tuning pegs on a ukulele are traditionally at right angles with the headstock, but you can find ukuleles set up in both ways.

Lesson 1: Let's make a start

Holding your ukulele

When learning to play any instrument it's important to hold it correctly. If you don't you will find that after playing it for a bit you will ache, or you will find some things unnecessarily difficult. You can play the ukulele sat down or stood up. It doesn't matter which, but look at the instructions below to make sure you're doing it right.

Sitting down

You should be sitting comfortably and relaxed on a chair with both feet flat on the floor.

Standing up

This is a bit harder at first as you have to get used to tucking the uke into your side – it should rest above your hip.

You might have to use your right forearm to keep the uke nestled into your side, but it shouldn't be forced – keep relaxed. Your left hand supports the other end of the ukulele, giving balance, and should be placed at the end of the fretboard ready to play some chords.

Tuning your ukulele

(5)

The ukulele can be tuned in several keys but for this tutor we will tune to G, C, E, A – the common 'C' tuning. The most common other tuning for a ukulele is in the key of D (using the notes A, D, F#, B).

We have provided tuning notes for your on the CD, so use the tuning pegs to tighten or loosen the strings to that they sound the same as the notes given.

6 - 9 **Tuning notes G, C, E and A**

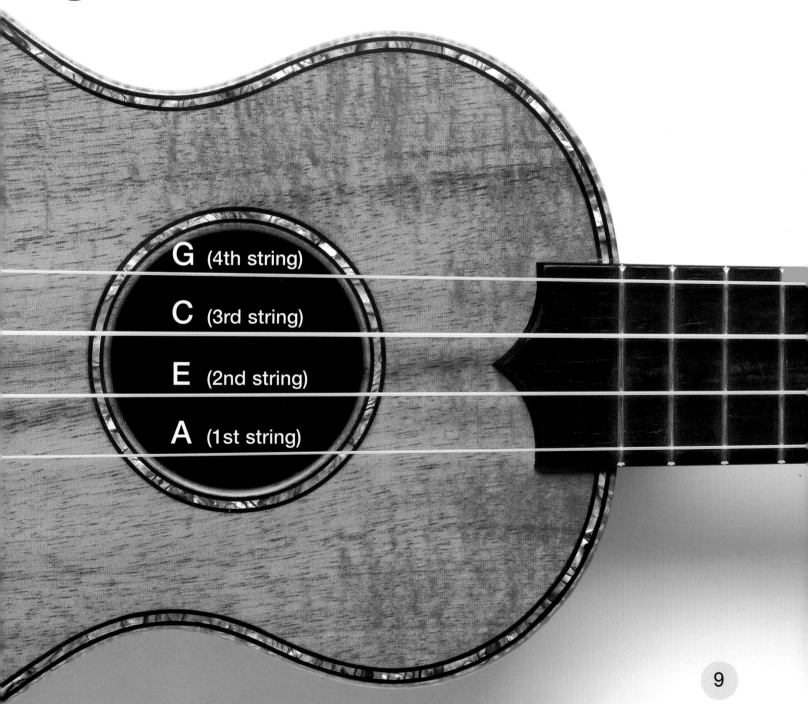

G (4th string)

C (3rd string)

E (2nd string)

A (1st string)

Playing chords

Chord 'window boxes' are used in both guitar and ukulele music to show you how to play different chords. The boxes are a grid reference to show where to place your fingers for each chord – the vertical lines represent the strings and the horizontal lines represent the frets.

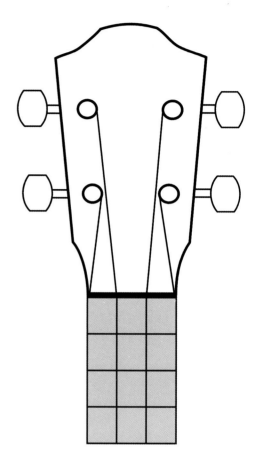

C chord

C

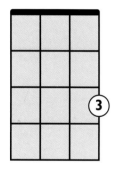

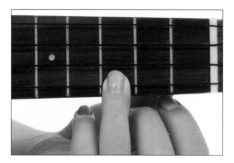

This box is saying place your third finger on the 1st string, just before the 3rd fret. Check the sound of your chord against the CD so you know you've got it right!

As a general rule it is better and faster to use your 1st finger for anything at the first fret, to use your second finger for anything at the 2nd fret and so forth.

Don't be tempted to use your first finger for a C chord. You may find it easier when you just need one finger, but eventually you will want to change chords very quickly and to do this your fingers need to be in order and not crossed.

F chord

F

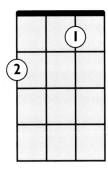 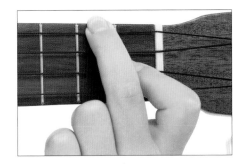

This box is saying place your first finger on the 2nd string, just before the 1st fret, and your second finger on the 4th string, just before the 2nd fret. Again, check the sound of your chord against the CD.

Thumb position

Some teachers will say that it is wrong to let your thumb rest above the fretboard and that it should rest behind the neck out of sight.

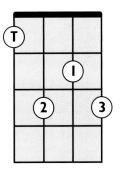 

I, along with plenty of players, don't agree with this. It's okay if your thumb sits quite high and is visible from the front. It will vary depending on what chord you are playing, some chord changes will mean the position of your thumb will move from over the neck to the middle of the neck as your wrist moves.

George Formby not only allowed his thumb to creep over the neck but sometimes he would use it in chord positions, as I do!

Here are two alternative ways of playing the same chord, one using the thumb:

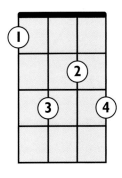 

The basic down-stroke

We've learned a chord – now we want to play it! There are many different ways to strum, and effects you can add, but it's basically about how you hit the strings. The most important and basic strum is the down-stroke. Get this right, and everything else should follow nicely.

The down-stroke is done by keeping the right hand nice and relaxed. Then strike the strings using the nail of your forefinger in a downwards motion.

Count 1,2,3,4 for every down-stroke. (Use a metronome if you have one, or count steadily yourself.)

TIP It is a good idea to keep the nails of your left hand short because this will help you hold down chords but you can allow the nails on your right hand to grow for strumming!

 # C Strum

Try strumming the chord of C for four beats (steady counts) and repeat this four times. In this book we will write this like this:

Time: **4/4**

The down arrow indicates that you should play a downstroke on the 1st beat of every four. We are writing it in four-beat units (we call these 'bars'), this is to make it easier to follow. It is better to play slowly at first! Learn the art of good timing rather than trying to play too fast and losing the steady beat.

 # F Strum

Try the same with the F chord.

Time: **4/4**

F

▼ | ▼ | ▼ | ▼ ‖
1 2 3 4 | 1 2 3 4 | 1 2 3 4 | 1 2 3 4

Changing chords

G7

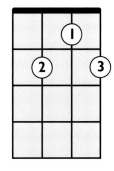 

To get started, let's look at two more chords we will use a lot, these are G7 and Am. Use the chord boxes and listen to the CD to check that you've got them right.

Am

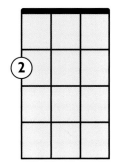 

Practise strumming each of these chords as you just did with the C and F chords, then practise strumming on every beat (the down arrow indicates a down-stroke). The CD demonstrates this on a C chord.

Down-beat strum

Time: **4/4**

We're now going to change chords and strum at the same time. We will practise this by playing *Sunrise*. It's a piece which we will keep coming back to in order to learn our different techniques, so you'll get to know it pretty well! Count 1, 2, 3, 4 for each chord and then change to the next and try not to leave a long gap between. The counts should just keep completely steady – like a ticking clock. When you have played this through twice, finish on a C chord.

Changing chords will get easier I promise; at first you will be slow and it might take a few seconds to get to the next chord but you will get faster. The more you practise the easier it will become for both your mind and your fingers! Nice 'n' slow then…

 ## Sunrise

Time: **4/4**

C	Am	F	G7
▼ ▼ ▼ ▼	▼ ▼ ▼ ▼	▼ ▼ ▼ ▼	▼ ▼ ▼ ▼
1 2 3 4	1 2 3 4	1 2 3 4	1 2 3 4

Lesson 2: Moving on

 Adding an up-stroke

The up-stroke is done with the fleshy tip of the finger and not the nail, starting at the 1st string and strumming back up to the top.

Let's try the exercise we've just done but this time we will add a quick up-stroke after the 4th beat and just before the 1st beat on the repeat. The stroke is shown by the up arrow. Here we go… play the whole piece twice, and don't forget to finish on a chord of C!

 Sunrise 2

Time: **4/4**

C				Am				F				G7			
▼	▼	▼	▼▲	▼	▼	▼	▼▲	▼	▼	▼	▼▲	▼	▼	▼	▼▲
1	2	3	4 +	1	2	3	4 +	1	2	3	4 +	1	2	3	4 +

At first your playing might have some pauses and hesitations in it but don't worry, you will get better and smoother. Listen to the demonstration a few more times and try again. Once you're happy with this exercise you are ready to move on to general strumming.

General strumming

We are now going to add an up-stroke after every down-stroke. This is almost like stroking the strings and creates a smooth strum. Remember to keep a relaxed wrist – as with all ukulele strokes the playing should come from your wrist and not your forearm. Imagine your wrist is broken – that's how loose it should be!

We will use the same chords again for this. The chord change comes on beat 1 so your fingers need to be ready on that chord before you play the down-stroke. Here it is – play it twice through as before.

 Sunrise 3

Time: **4/4**

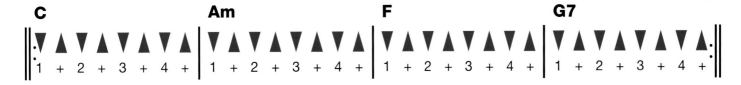

 When you're confident, let's up the tempo and play it a bit faster.

By The Rivers Of Babylon

This song uses three of the chords we have just learned, and a couple of different strumming patterns. Follow the arrows, listen to the CD and play – you're doing great!

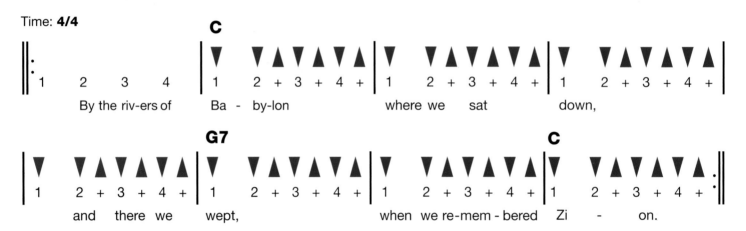

The demonstration you will listen to on the CD plays the strums on beat 3 very quietly, and on the repeat adds an up-stroke between beats 1 and 2. You could try this, or experiment with the strumming pattern yourself, add your own unique flavour to your music!

Lesson 3: Accents and new chords

 Light and shade ('accents')

An accent is where we hit the strings a bit louder on a particular strum. Accents are a key feature of music, giving shape to melodies and rhythms. This also means they're important in establishing different 'grooves' – if everything was playing at the same volume and given the same importance the music would have no shape. We add accents to break up sequences, giving interest and variety to our playing.

We will try putting an accent on every 1st beat – hit the down-stroke a bit harder and then return to the normal volume for the other strokes. The 1st beat still has the same length but is just louder so don't pause, just make it stand out. You will see that the accented strums are indicated by a horizontal line above the arrow.

 Sunrise 4

Off we go… twice through

Time: **4/4**

Excellent – keep practising and listening to the CD!

Also practise playing some strums quieter than others – remember you are the boss so experiment with your ukulele and see what you sounds and effects you create!

Lesson 3: Accents and new chords

 The following songs use a mixture of up-strokes and down-strokes. Follow the arrows, listen to the CD and see how different combinations of strokes can create different feels.

Before you start these pieces practice each new chord on its own, strumming up and down, before playing them in the songs. (Also have a recap of any chords which we learned earlier.)

D

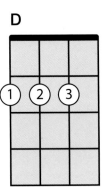 

A7

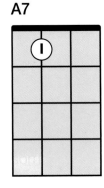 

 ## Hush Little Baby

This classic song is quite soft and so requires a smooth strum. To create a smooth sound, avoid any strong accents to make your strumming very gentle and even.

Time: **4/4**

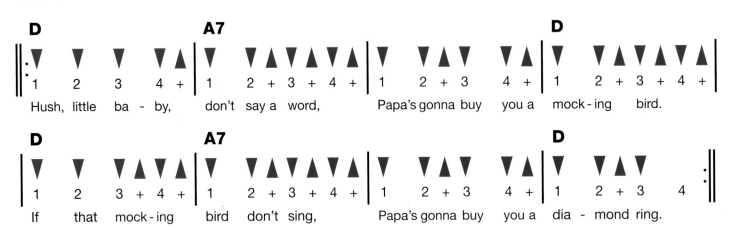

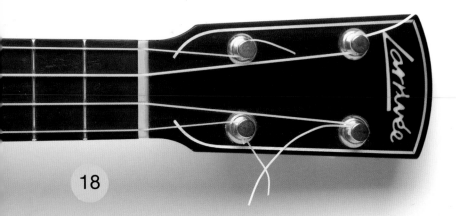

18

Here are the new chords you will need for *Down By The Riverside.*

C7

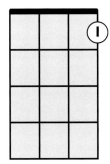 

E7

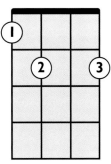 

G

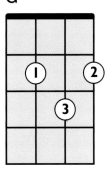 

36 -37 Down By The Riverside

This song is much more upbeat, and has a very rhythmic feel. We therefore want to add some accented strokes and we do these on beats 2 and 4. These are the off-beats, the weaker beats of a bar. This technique of accented off-beats is a key feature of reggae music.

Time: **4/4**

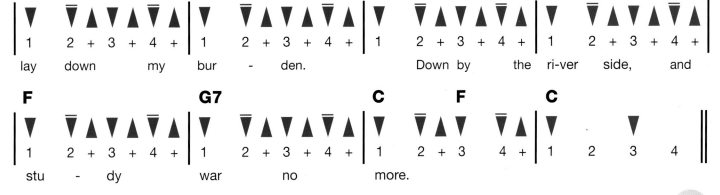

Lesson 4: You're doing great!

 Stretching exercise

Before looking at some more challenging chords try an exercise to loosen the left hand and get used to stretching, becoming more supple and finding our way around the fretboard.

We will play a short scale on each string, using each finger to play from the 1st fret to the 4th fret, and then back down. The string can either be plucked with the index finger or the thumb. Use the finger that corresponds correctly to each fret: first finger on the 1st fret, second finger on the 2nd fret. Pluck each note once.

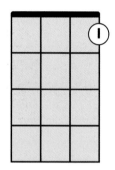 

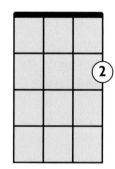 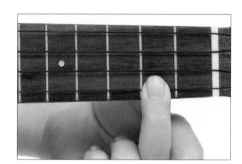

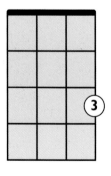 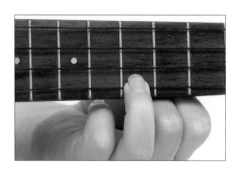

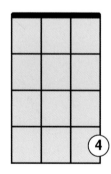 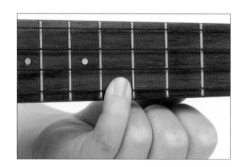

Once you are confident, extend this pattern and play it on all four strings. Start on the first string and play the sequence twice on each string before moving on to the next:

Sequence 1 - play twice

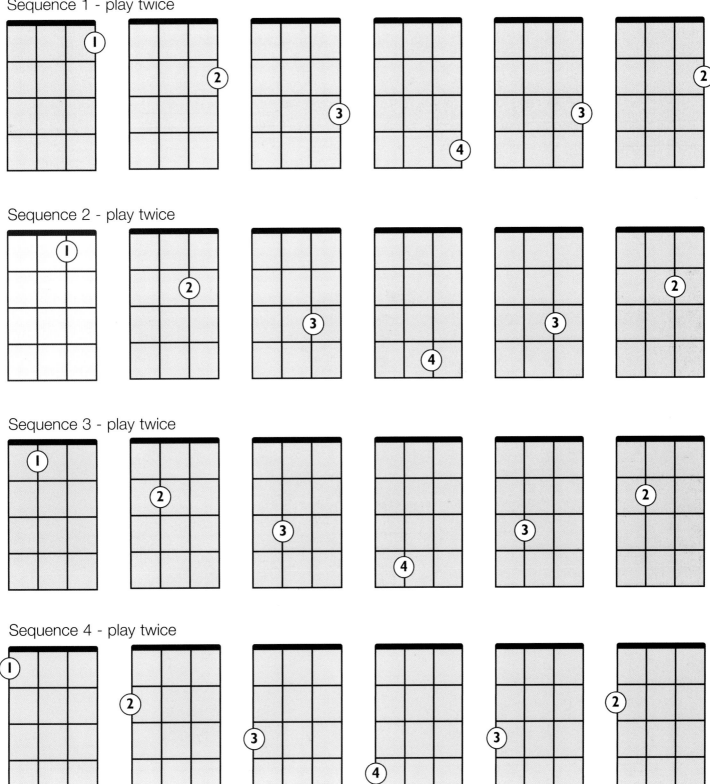

Sequence 2 - play twice

Sequence 3 - play twice

Sequence 4 - play twice

39 **Some harder chords**

These chords are more challenging but they often appear in pop songs and old 'standards' so they are certainly worth learning.

There might be some chords that take weeks before you get them to sound clean. If there is buzzing or a dead sound it is probably because you are not pressing down hard enough on the string or your finger is actually or than just before the fret.

Practise making every chord sound clean. Eventually they will, although with certain chords you may have to put up with a slight buzzing until your fingers get used to the chord shapes – persevere. Some chords took me ages to get sounding right – I simply played them as well as I could for many weeks until eventually I didn't find them so hard!

40

Scarborough Fair

Time: **3/4**

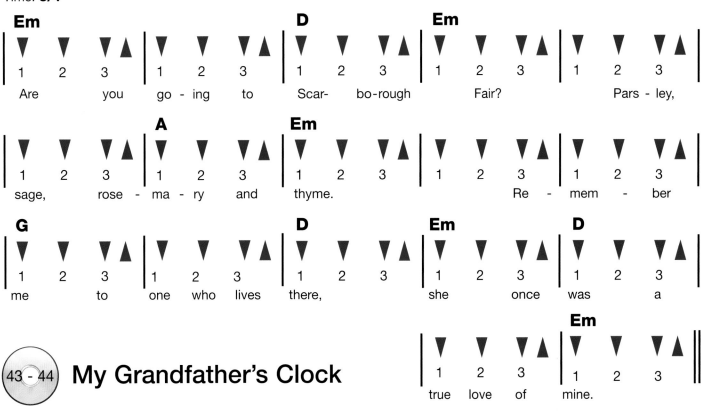

Are you go - ing to Scar- bo-rough Fair? Pars - ley,
sage, rose - ma - ry and thyme. Re - mem - ber
me to one who lives there, she once was a
true love of mine.

My Grandfather's Clock

Time: **4/4**

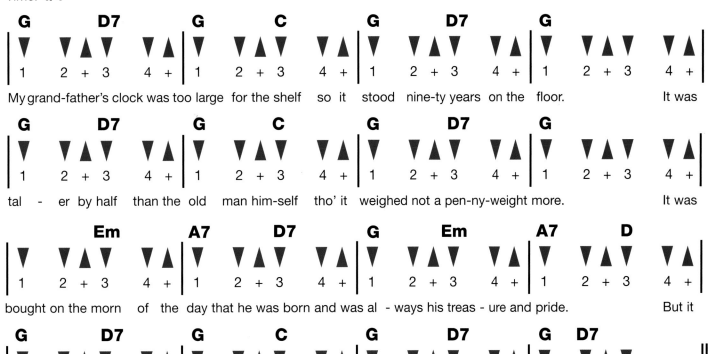

My grand-father's clock was too large for the shelf so it stood nine-ty years on the floor. It was
tal - er by half than the old man him-self tho' it weighed not a pen-ny-weight more. It was
bought on the morn of the day that he was born and was al - ways his treas - ure and pride. But it
stopped short never to go a-gain when the old man died.

Lesson 5: Rock 'n' roll riffing

(45) Sometimes small changes in chord shapes can make dramatic differences to the music, and that's what happens in these Rock 'n' Roll pieces. This exercise is good for the left hand as it involves taking the finger off and putting it back on fairly often – it's a good exercise to keep revisiting, and a lot of fun!

For every chord follow the strum symbols. Generally, a down-stroke and an up-stroke is played for each box. Watch out for accents and a slightly longer note at the end of each line – just strike the down-stroke a little harder and give it some welly!

Rock 'n' Roll

Try playing this very slowly at first and be sure to get
the riff in your head as this will make it so much easier.
Once you're confident, try it fast – it's a lot of fun!
Finish on an F at the very end.

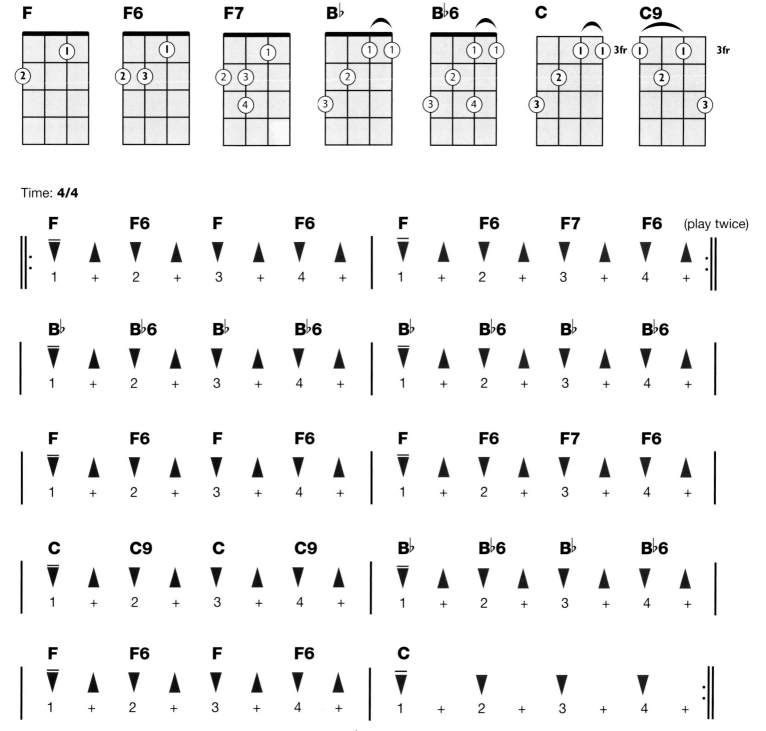

Note: F6 is the same chord shape as Dm, and B♭6 is the same shape as Gm.

Lesson 6: Hawaiian stroke

 48 The Hawaiian stroke

This is a fun (and simple) stroke.
I call it the Hawaiian stroke because I've seen
many Hawaiian ukulele players use it (or something
very similar). It lifts the song and adds interest
to the strumming pattern. Really it's a simple
up- and down-stroke but usually the accent is
on the up-stroke.

Hawaiian Stroke

Time: **4/4**

Going back to *Sunrise* let's have a look at this and
get to grips with this new stroke. Keep listening to
the CD and practising.

 49 -50 Sunrise Hawaiian

Time: **4/4**

Now we can try to add the pattern to *Jingle Bells*!

 (51 - 52) **Jingle Bells**

Time: **4/4**

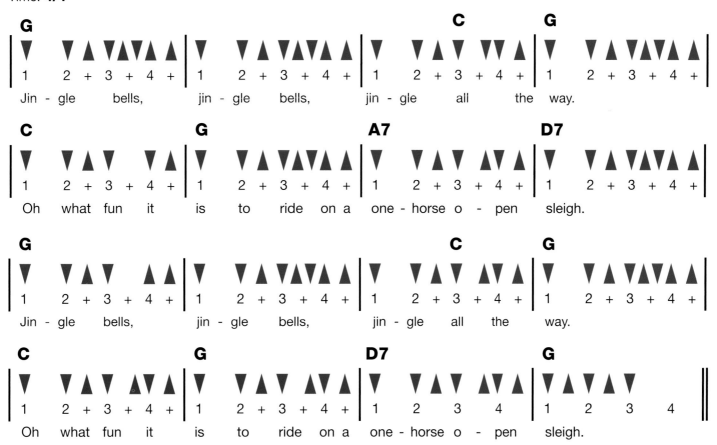

> **TIP** Watch as many ukulele players as you can. I found it helpful to join the Ukulele Society and the Formby Society – clubs are great things to join as you can learn from others. Experiment with your own ideas too since the ukulele has many possibilities!

Lesson 7: Fingerpicking

 53 I hope this book has provided some insights into developing your own unique style of playing. Before we finish, we're going to look at two new techniques: fingerpicking and the split-stroke, which is also sometimes known as the 'Formby' or 'syncopated' stroke.

Whatever technique you learn, it is always important to bring your own style to it. No two players ever play the same, even if they have had the same teacher – everyone has different influences, tastes, personalities and fingers! A solo can vary every time I play it because the techniques learned are a recipe which can be varied – I can choose to add more of one ingredient than another.

The most important thing is that you become happy with the strokes you've learned and you decide when, where and how often to use them. Some songs are best using fingerpicking, some suit strumming better and some need a bit of both!

Fingerpicking

Fingerpicking is where you pluck individual strings in a repetitive pattern. There are many ways to fingerpick and many different patterns you can use, but this version works particularly well on the ukulele.

 54 - 55 ## A Fingerpicking Sunrise

Use the thumb and index finger and pluck the strings in this order: 1, 4, 2, 3, 2, 4. Alternate between the index finger (I) and thumb (T), follow the diagram below:

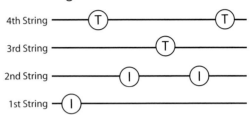

Now, do this but playing the chord of C.

It may help to think that your index finger is playing the 1st and 2nd strings, and your thumb is playing the 3rd and 4th strings. Start slowly at first and gradually increase in speed, keep repeating the cycle and there you have fingerpicking!

Now let's try the pattern within *Sunrise* – you now know it well so should only have to think about your right hand! We will play the pattern through twice on each chord before changing.

Fingerpicking
Time: **3/4**

C		Am	
‖: 1 4 2 3 2 4	1 4 2 3 2 4	1 4 2 3 2 4	1 4 2 3 2 4

F		G7	
1 4 2 3 2 4	1 4 2 3 2 4	1 4 2 3 2 4	1 4 2 3 2 4 :‖

Did you notice how *A Fingerpicking Sunrise* only had three beats in each bar? The pattern of fingerpicking we have learned works very well with pieces which have three beats in every bar, and also those with a more laid-back feel. *Silent Night,* the famous Christmas carol tune by Franz Gruber, is one such piece. As always, start slowly!

 Silent Night

Fingerpicking
Time: **3/4**

C				**G**
1 4 2 3 2 4	1 4 2 3 2 4	1 4 2 3 2 4	1 4 2 3 2 4	1 4 2 3 2 4
Si - lent night,		ho - ly night,		all is

C	**C**	**F**		
1 4 2 3 2 4	1 4 2 3 2 4	1 4 2 3 2 4	1 4 2 3 2 4	1 4 2 3 2 4
calm,	all is bright.	Round yon	vir - gin,	

C	**F**		**C**	
1 4 2 3 2 4	1 4 2 3 2 4	1 4 2 3 2 4	1 4 2 3 2 4	1 4 2 3 2 4
moth - er and	child,	ho - ly	in - fant so	ten - der and

G	**E7**	**Am**	**D**	
1 4 2 3 2 4	1 4 2 3 2 4	1 4 2 3 2 4	1 4 2 3 2 4	1 4 2 3 2 4
mild.	Sleep in	heav - en- ly	peace.	

C	**G**	**C**	
1 4 2 3 2 4	1 4 2 3 2 4	1 4 2 3 2 4	1 4 2 3 2 4 :
Sleep in	heav - en- ly	peace.	

 TIP Now think of any of your favourite songs and see if you can get hold of the chords and see if fingerpicking will work well! It's always good to discover new songs.

Lesson 8: The split-stroke (Formby stroke)

 It would be possible to write half a book alone dedicated to the split-stroke. This stroke is one of the most requested techniques for any fan of George Formby.

The split stroke is called that because the strumming is 'split' or, in musical terms, 'syncopated' which means breaking the rhythm.

George Formby had a fantastic strumming style and heavily influenced the technique (even though it was around before his rise to fame). We could get technical on this subject but all I'd like to do is give you a basic introduction to the stroke. You can use it as an ingredient and vary how you use it to fit the song you're playing.

Formby played the split-stroke in at least three different ways. The normal way is what we will learn, but he also sometimes played just after the beat, or anticipated the beat.

The essential strum pattern is a sequence of seven, and we will try the pattern on the chord of C. This is how it sounds:

Split-stroke

Time: **4/4**

▼ Down = strike all strings with nail (accent).

▼ Down = strike all strings with nail (accent).

▲ Up = upstrum with fleshy part of finger (mainly hitting the 1st string).

▼ Down = this time just striking the top string (TS) but you will probably catch the next string as well – that's ok.

▼ Down = strike all strings (accent).

▲ Up = upstrum (mainly hitting the 1st string).

▼ Down = again, just striking the top string.

This is the trickiest stroke in the book so be patient and listen to the CD to get the pattern embedded in your mind. The up-strokes are quite light and are almost accidental as your wrist comes back into position for the next down-stroke. Sometimes it is easier to try looking at it in two sections. Master 'Down, Down, Up' before working on 'TS, Down, Up, TS'. When you think you're confident with it in two sections, put the two together to make the complete sequence. Best to take it so slowly, like on the CD.

This stroke must come from the wrist, which must be incredibly relaxed, and not the forearm.

We'll now work the technique into an exercise. And guess which? Yes, *Sunrise* again – you've already got a lot to think about here! Look at the accents on the full downstrokes and remember to play these strokes pretty hard.

Keep repeating it until you're really secure, but don't forget to keep relaxed. This stroke needs a careful balance between feeling so relaxed it is like you have a broken wrist and at the same time being in total control of the music and your ukulele! You are always boss of your instrument and this stroke does need some attack!

 A Split-stroke Sunrise

Time: **4/4**

C	Am	F	G7
▼ ▼▲▼▼▲▼	▼ ▼▲▼▼▲▼	▼ ▼▲▼▼▲▼	▼ ▼▲▼▼▲▼
1 + 2 + 3 + 4 +	1 + 2 + 3 + 4 +	1 + 2 + 3 + 4 +	1 + 2 + 3 + 4 +

Lesson 9: Left-hand techniques

 Dampening

Now and again it's nice to give your playing some more colour by shortening the full sound of a chord and dampening the strings to achieve a more percussive sound to the strumming rhythm.

To do this you simply release the pressure on your fingertips and then reapply the usual pressure, release again etc. Your fingers almost leave the strings. It's particularly useful on *Highly Overrated*, which we'll look at later in the book, as the chords lend themselves to the technique.

Listen to the CD – I'm vamping on a G chord so have a listen and experiment.

 Tapping

This is another effect you can have a play with. It's usually applied to chords that include a finger on the first string.

Everytime there is an up-stroke, take off the finger that is on the first string but put back down in position ready for the down-stroke that follows. We have marked this on the music by an asterisk. You can hear this on the CD.

To grasp the 'tapping' take a look at this little riff:

 A Tapping Sunrise

Time: **4/4**

| C | | | Am | | | F | | | G7 | | |

```
   C           *         *   | Am          *         *   | F           *         *   | G7          *         *
|: ▼   ▼ ▲ ▼ ▼ ▲ ▼ | ▼   ▼ ▲ ▼ ▼ ▲ ▼ | ▼   ▼ ▲ ▼ ▼ ▲ ▼ | ▼   ▼ ▲ ▼ ▼ ▲ ▼ :|
   1 + 2 + 3 + 4 +   1 + 2 + 3 + 4 +   1 + 2 + 3 + 4 +   1 + 2 + 3 + 4 +
```

> **TIP** Listen to as much George Formby playing as possible, especially the slower songs because they allow you to hear the split-stroke clearly. Formby played very fast – when I was a young player I used to slow records down on a turntable to hear his style. That's not easy these days with mp3s and CDs, so pick slower songs like *TT Race* and *Chinese Laundry Blues,* and listen out for the uke solo – can you hear the tapping and syncopation?

She'll Be Coming Round The Mountain

This song is ideal to see how the split-stroke and ordinary strumming can be used together.
If you find it tricky, just do whatever strumming you think suits the song and enjoy playing!
You can always come back to this stroke at another time.

Time: **4/4**

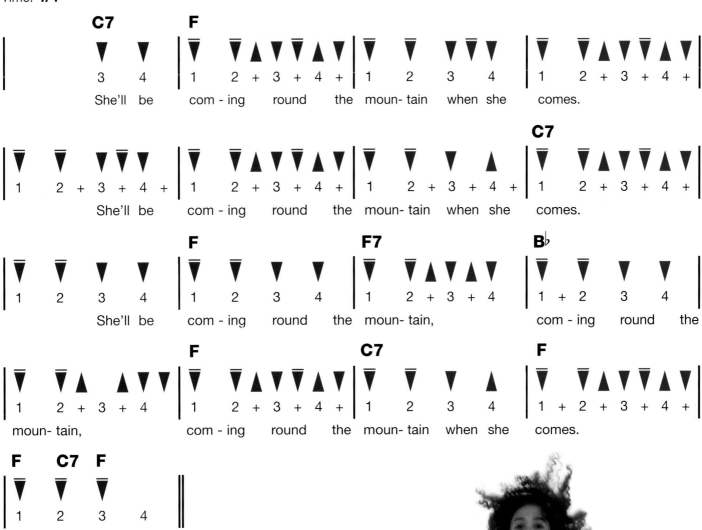

Lesson 10: Show off!

68 - 69 Well done! You're at the end. To finish the book, here's a song of mine called *Highly Overrated*. There are a few new chords, but nothing too tricky, and the verse is very simple, so if you hesitate, just join back in for that riff!

The strumming pattern on *Highly Overrated* works really well with the Hawaiian stroke. If you're happy with this, why not give it a try using the Hawaiian technique we've learned? If not, just strum simply and enjoy playing the chords!

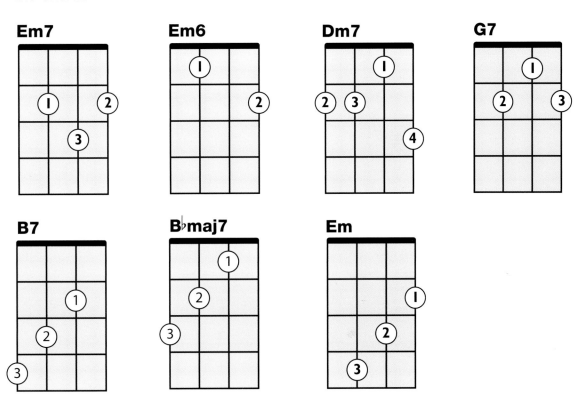

Highly Overrated

Time: **4/4**

Em7 |▼▲▼▲▼▲▼▲| 1 + 2 + 3 + 4 +
Em6 |▼▲▼▲▼▲▼▲| 1 + 2 + 3 + 4 +
Em7 |▼▲▼▲▼▲▼▲| 1 + 2 + 3 + 4 +
Em6 |▼▲▼▲▼▲▼▲| 1 + 2 + 3 + 4 +

Are you stressed?　　　　　　　In a　mess?　　　　　　Not at all

Em7 |▼▲▼▲▼▲▼▲| 1 + 2 + 3 + 4 +
Em6 |▼▲▼▲▼▲▼▲| 1 + 2 + 3 + 4 +
Dm7 |▼▲▼▲▼▲▼▲| 1 + 2 + 3 + 4 +
G7 |▼▲▼▲▼▲▼▲| 1 + 2 + 3 + 4 +

blessed,　　　　　　Not a　high card　left in your　hand.　　　May-be

Em7 |▼▲▼▲▼▲▼▲| 1 + 2 + 3 + 4 +
Em6 |▼▲▼▲▼▲▼▲| 1 + 2 + 3 + 4 +
Em7 |▼▲▼▲▼▲▼▲| 1 + 2 + 3 + 4 +
Em6 |▼▲▼▲▼▲▼▲| 1 + 2 + 3 + 4 +

time,　　　　　　to step　back　　　　　from a long rail-road

Em7 |▼▲▼▲▼▲▼▲| 1 + 2 + 3 + 4 +
Em6 |▼▲▼▲▼▲▼▲| 1 + 2 + 3 + 4 +
Dm7 |▼　▼　▼　▼| 1 + 2 + 3 + 4 +
G7 |▼　▼　▼　▼| 1 + 2 + 3 + 4 +

track,　　　　　　see this　ghost train　of a　journ - ey　for　what it

Em7 |▼▲▼▲▼▲▼▲| 1 + 2 + 3 + 4 +
Em6 |▼▲▼▲▼▲▼▲| 1 + 2 + 3 + 4 +
Em7 |▼▲▼▲▼▲▼▲| 1 + 2 + 3 + 4 +
Em6 |▼▲▼▲▼▲▼▲| 1 + 2 + 3 + 4 +

is…

Em7 |▼▲▼▲▼▲▼▲| 1 + 2 + 3 + 4 +
Em6 |▼▲▼▲▼▲▼▲| 1 + 2 + 3 + 4 +
Dm7 |▼▲▼▲▼▲▼▲| 1 + 2 + 3 + 4 +
G7 |▼▲▼▲▼▲▼▲| 1 + 2 + 3 + 4 +

Em |▼　▼　▼　▼| 1 + 2 + 3 + 4 +
B7 |▼　▼　▼　▼| 1 + 2 + 3 + 4 +
B♭maj7 |▼　▼　▼　▼| 1 + 2 + 3 + 4 +
A |▼　▼　▼　▼| 1 + 2 + 3 + 4 +

You　try hard to　sleep but there's ten other things　all　fight-ing　for your time.

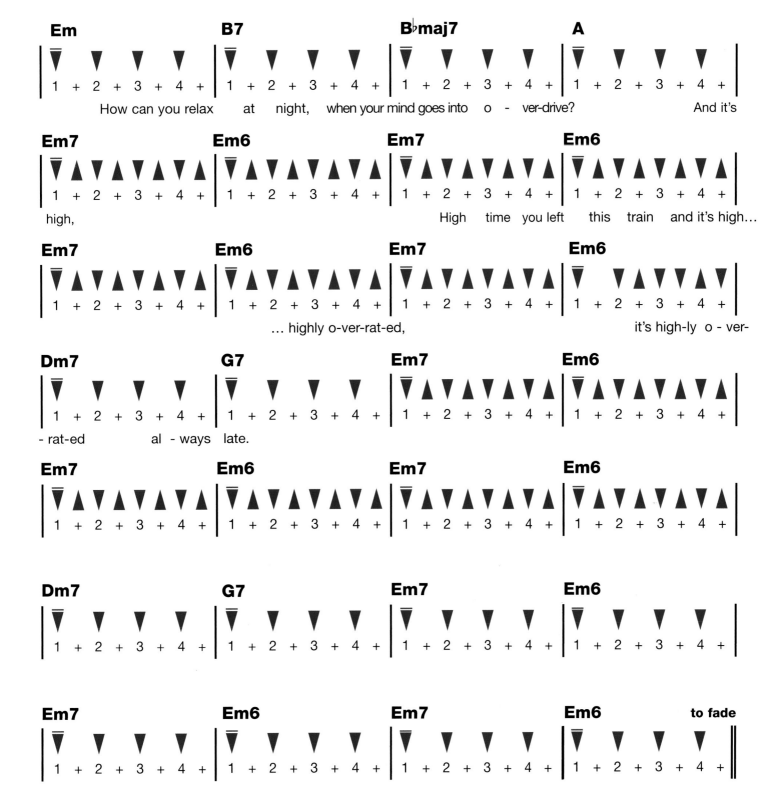

Further Info

George Formby

Probably the most influential and renowned ukulele player, George Formby was, at the peak of his 40-year career, one of the most famous entertainers in the British Isles. He became well known for his own brand of northern humour which he communicated most famously through his performance of songs using his banjo ukulele (or 'banjolele' – see page 5 for further info!), a hybrid instrument combining the Hawaiian ukulele and the American banjo.

Formby wrote and performed over 300 songs during his career, touring the country and appearing in numerous films. During the war he continued his work by travelling throughout Europe to boost the morale of the troops. His most famous songs include, *The Window Cleaner*, *Fanlight Fanny* and *Leaning On A Lamp Post*. He died in 1961 at the age of 56.

Further ukulele information

Below are some websites which might inspire you, help you, or give you some further details about the ukulele and key players of the instrument.

Societies, meetings, workshops and conventions

The Ukulele Society – www.usgb.co.uk
The George Formby Society –
www.georgeformby.co.uk

Collectable old ukes for sale

John Croft 'The Ukuleleman' –
www.theukuleleman.com
Andy Eastwood – www.andyeastwood.com

Ukulele web forum

www.ukulelecosmos.com

Uke heroes & ambassadors

The Ukulele Orchestra –
www.ukuleleorchestra.com
James Hill – www.ukulelejames.com
Elias Sibley – www.sibley-music.com
Peter Moss
Gabriella La Foley
Ray Bernard – Long established statesman
of the ukulele and instrument expert.
Andy Eastwood – www.andyeastwood.com

About the author

Steven Sproat is a ukulele player based in Gloucestershire with considerable experience, having been heard on many radio stations including BBC Radio 2, BBC Scotland, Severn Sound and Manx Radio. In his career spanning 20 years, he has played in prestigious venues such as Ronnie Scott's (London), St David's Hall (Exeter), at the Cheltenham Festival and at the New York Ukulele Festival. Steven is also active as a teacher, with his most famous pupil being comedian Harry Hill. Steven is establishing a Cheltenham & Gloucester Ukulele Studio for group and individual lessons, hoping to have workshops and ukulele guests to share their skills and performance. Feel free to email him at sproatie@btinternet.com or check his website for latest news: www.stevensproat.com.

Track listing and about the CD

The CD included contains spoken instructions and demonstrations to help you learn; it's like having your very own teacher! It demonstrates what the various techniques are supposed to sound like so you can listen carefully and match them up with your own playing. The CD also contains full demonstrations of all pieces, plus backing tracks without the ukulele, so you can play along on your own. The first time you hear the piece, it will be the full demonstration, the second time will be the backing track only.

Have fun!

Track

1	The wonderful world of ukes
2	The uke family
3	A few ideas you might find useful

Lesson 1 – Let's make a start

4	Holding your ukulele
5	Tuning your ukulele
6	Tuning note 'G'
7	Tuning note 'C'
8	Tuning note 'E'
9	Tuning note 'A'
10	Playing chords
11	C chord
12	F chord
13	The basic down-stroke
14	C Strum
15	F Strum
16	Changing chords (includes chords G7 and Am)
17	Down-beat strum
18-19	Sunrise

Lesson 2 – Moving on

20	Adding an up-stroke
21-22	Sunrise 2
23-24	Sunrise 3
25-26	And faster now...
27-28	By The Rivers Of Babylon

Lesson 3 – Accents and new chords

29	Light and shade ('accents')
30-31	Sunrise 4
32	Chords D and A7
33-34	Hush Little Baby
35	Chords C7, E7 and G
36-37	Down By The Riverside

Lesson 4 – You're doing great!

38	Stretching Exercise
39	Some harder chords
40	Chords A, D7, Em and E'
41-42	Scarborough Fair
43-44	My Grandfather's Clock

Lesson 5 – Rock 'n' roll riffing

45	Introduction
46-47	Rock 'n' Roll

Lesson 6 – Hawaiian stroke

48	The Hawaiian stroke
49-50	Sunrise Hawaiian
51-52	Jingle Bells

Lesson 7 – Fingerpicking

53	Introduction
54-55	A Fingerpicking Sunrise
56-57	Silent Night

Lesson 8 – The split-stroke

58	Introduction
59	Split-stroke
60-61	A split-stroke Sunrise

Lesson 9 – Left hand techniques

62	Dampening
63	Tapping
64-65	A Tapping Sunrise
66-67	She'll Be Coming Round The Mountain

Lesson 10 – Show off!

68	Well done!
69	Highly Overrated